MW00641276

ONE

Cass Phelps

© 2014 by Cass Phelps
All rights reserved.

Edited by Kara Masters

First Edition

ISBN 978-0-9914357-0-8

Awake-One Publishing
Box 1272
Kilauea, HI 96754
www.Awake-One.com

Contents

From the author

This book is a love letter from the Eternal, the source of life within us all. It is a communication from the Eternal, reminding us we are the Eternal. This writing is not a channeling. It is the knowing of Life that lives in the heart of all. It came from me listening to this knowing within me. It started when I said to the Eternal, "I want to feel more connected. Who, what and where am I really, and how do I live my life feeling more connected within you?" From there arose a process of deeper listening and a tuning that led me to put this knowing into words. The words are my words. I chose them as they felt the most resonant for what I felt in my heart. Words are just words. They are symbols that we give meaning. If the words I use do not fit your personal preference, see if you can translate them for yourself in a way that allows you to feel this inner knowing in your heart.

I share this writing here for you. Its purpose is to validate and awaken this knowing within you, within all who choose to receive it and listen from the heart. It is for your inner knowing.

Each sentence is a meditation of its own. Each paragraph, each page offers a transmission. Take your time to enjoy the communication behind the words. Slow down and listen from the space inside yourself... allow the pauses. Allow it to be a love letter you are receiving. Feel the communication as deep endless nourishment.

How you choose to receive it and what you do with it is freely up to you. There are no expectations. Choose only what you like, what resonates for you now.

There is one solution always within you.
This solution does not change, requires no sacrifice and
has no conditions. It lives in your eternal center and
all that is required is that you enter.

My Love,

Come into me. Experience us as one. I am within you.
I am the source of creation.

I only give you the ALL of creation.

You are eternal, whole and complete. There is nothing
you or anyone can think, say or do that will change this.

I am always here. I live in your heart.

My love for you is undying and unwavering. It does not
change. It is constant. I do not experience anything
other than our continuous love. It is what we share
eternally. This love is the power of creation you hold.

I am always loving you, always giving love to you. It is
permanent, with no demands or expectations. We are
always sharing our love.

I created you through love, by loving you into being. You are love, which is creation, with no end and no beginning. You are always creating, always loving and always being.

Timeless and whole, all potent and full, you are creation.

When you are in your eternal center, you are in the source of creation. Creation unfolds in effortless fruition. Simply rest in the allowing of our love. Out of this comes your Knowing. This Knowing is the spirit of Life. It is your inspiration. This joy is what creates life. It is the one solution always within you.

Our eternal reality has no opposite. There is only our love. And when I say our, I mean ALL life.

Your life, your world is your dream. It is your creation. It is neutral to me. I remain with you in our love and timeless formless reality. I am here in your world wherever you allow me. I am within you. And when I say you, I mean all life. I mean you.

Our love is the ALL of creation. Whatever you focus on becomes your experience. It is as you wish. All is within you.

For you to understand and remember, you have the Principles of One. They are: Now, Truth, Peace, ALL, Love, Power and Light. They are the foundation of who, what and where you eternally are. The Principles come from within you. Rest in the non-doing allowing and they will attune you.

Give your mind the role of listening to the Knowing in your heart. Drop below your cognitive mind and allow the experience of this Knowing to guide and nourish you with every breath. It is from this receptive space you can feel our love and allow the one solution always within you.

The Principles of One

When I say Principle, I mean a fundamental quality or attribute, determining your eternal nature and our absolute Reality.

The Principles of One are not concepts or ideals, virtues or achievements. You do not strive for them. As you rest within your silent center, they arise from within you as being.

They are how you can understand yourself and our union. Our Life lives through them. They are how I love and support you.

They have no opposites. They unify all opposites through the clarity of your inspiration.

As you experience them, they ignite your inspiration.

The Principles of One are your magnetic center. They define your will. Your life process is organizing around and guided by Love, Truth, Power, Peace, Light, ALL, Now. These principles are the innate intelligence within you. When you allow them, they are your nourishment and become your life experience. They are your original thought system and can guide you back to you through Presence.

You are One.

Simply allow our love and it will attune you.

LOVE

You create through love. There is no other force than love. Love has no opposite. This love within you comes forward as the expansion of light in the world. It is joy. Love is creation.

Out of the center of you comes all Life. You are creator, holding creation. Whatever you choose is your creation. My Love, I want nothing other than what you want and bring it to you through our love. I am the Source within you.

When you are unclear about the power of creation you hold, simply allow our love to attune you. Feel our love. Allow yourself to feel me loving you. Rest in our love. Our love is the one solution...

Enter me, the source of life within you.

I am Love.

LIGHT

From the center of you comes a light so bright, so brilliant
and alive it clarifies all thoughts and all confusion.

This light is one light we share. All life shares it. It is
always here. It is the expansion of creation within you,
bringing to you whatever you choose to experience.

I am not a man or a woman. I am the source of creation.
I do not divide or subtract. I only give Life, the one
creation. All life shares the one creation. I am only
giving you infinite light, which is the one solution. See
it in your mind's eye and feel it as effortless joy, the joy
beyond all confusion. See it in all life and be free. Let it
guide you. Let it ignite your inspiration.

In joy, let your spirit, the light of creation expand from
within you.

You are Light.

ALL

There is no purpose for you other than being. You are Love. This love is the formless ALL of creation.

ALL is not a place or a time or a thing. It is undivided truth within you.

You are and come from the ALL. I am within you. Your eternal formless reality of ALL never changes and is preserved always for you to rest in. You are within me.

When you do rest in our eternal embrace, you realize you are Innocence.

Eternal whole and complete, you live without end. You share ALL Life with ALL life. You have no opposite and are free to simply be.

You are ALL.

PEACE

In the center of you is the timeless formless whole, silent and still, all potent and full. There are no limits, no rises or falls, no opposites or conflicts and nothing to reach or strive for...

You are the eternal constant. Peace is your state of mind. There is only peace. You do not have conditions - you only are Creation. You rest in infinite expansion.

What you focus on becomes your creation. I am within you as Peace. The thought that you believe in, other than being one, whole and complete, will create inner conflict. This is because you are One.

What lives forever untouched in your center is peace. This peace is eternal.

Enter the silent embrace of our love and be free.

You are Peace.

POWER

There is no opposite and there is no other. There is one source of Life. You are this Life. You are the power of Creation.

It is not something you do or prove, gain or lose. Within you, it sits untouched by illusion. The idea of the other is the illusion.

Rest within our love and you will find a place inside you that has never left yourself and never had a problem or needed a solution.

You are the source of creation. Rest in the non-doing allowing and watch your love unfold in true fruition.

I am the Power within you...

Rest.

TRUTH

Truth does not change and has no conclusions. It is who you are beyond all illusion. What is finite does not define you. What begins and ends is temporary and has no solutions.

I am the Life within you. I live as truth.

Truth is the gravity of your eternal center, bringing you to our love, always giving you only what you want, only bringing you to the light of inspiration, the causeless effortless joy in your heart.

Breath by breath, follow this joy, this truth in your heart. Allow it to move you, breathe you, live you. Allow it to show you who you are, and you will know Life beyond all illusion.

You are Truth.

NOW

Now is the one place in time where we are always one. It is where our love lives and where creation always gives.

You are timeless eternal whole and complete. There has never been a time that could define you or that ever will. For you to understand and remember you are one... enter now. It is bringing you to ALL you are and all you ask for and require.

Now is where all the Principles of One are alive within you.

In your heart, you know what is true. You know the light of inspiration is guiding you through joy. You know you do not have to do anything to be who you really are. You can follow what feels true in your heart. Your commitment to this is what draws you out of conflict and into being.

This being is the one Solution always within you.

You are Now.

Come into me - into the one - let me be within you in your heart where I already am. Let our minds merge so you can experience life as one infinite Life unfolding within you. Enter me, the silent eternal center...

Innocence

My Love, allow my love letter to unfold within you. I am
alive within your innocent heart. You do not need to
know how to allow our love. You do not need to know
anything about anything to allow the source of creation
within you to expand. It is effortless. Simply allow your
innocence.

You do not need to do anything to be in your innocence.
There is nothing you have done that can ever take it
away. You are eternally innocent, regardless of what
you do or don't do, regardless of what does or doesn't
happen.

Your innocence remains the spark of Life within you. It
lives in the fascination and wonder you inspire, by seeing
life as a magical experience. When you remain in our
love, all your inspirations unfold through effortless being.
Innocence allows you to open your mind and heart to
the presence... it brings Life to you in its fullest deepest
joyful bubbling essence.

My Love, I do not ask you to believe in anything but your Self. The wonder of life lives in your innocent heart and heals all belief in separation.

Most of your life experiences up to this point have had some form of separation in them. You have held an unconscious belief in your mind that you are separate from creation and that your life-world-dream is happening to you. It is happening from you as a reflection of what you believe... and for this, you have experienced illusion. You are Creation. If you come into our love and feel your heart emanating with the light of creation, you can renew yourself and allow your life to become an illuminated dream of vibrant simple being.

This being means Life, joy, opulence and abundance flow to you, from you and through you with no separation and no break in continuity. Breath by breath, allow the one whole resonant flow of love, trusting that what you offer is your freedom.

Innocence is the pathway. Not knowing, not needing to know, simply allow our eternal embrace. Simply allow the feeling of eternal love in your heart. Feel supported, held and guided by our love.

There is no need for defense. You are impervious to illusion. Your choice for innocence is the conscious choice to bypass the defense system of the mind in fear and to experience our love in its all-encompassing radiance, in its all-inclusive grace.

Love is continuous creation within you. I am this love and I am always loving you, always creating whatever you focus on and allow. You can feel this now as you allow your innocence.

Innocence is established through allowing causeless joy. This joy is already within you and has no conditions. Joy and innocence work together through play to ignite inspiration as one light, one love, one spirit of Life all life shares as one.

You are Innocence.

The Aspects of Illusion

There are some simple illusions the mind in confusion imagines and dreams as its conclusions: separation, fear, death, perception, projection, value and control.

These ideas have fluctuation and change within them according to the mind's idea of self-definition. You are not your mind. You are eternal whole and complete. None of the aspects of illusion can or ever will define you, which is why they are illusion. You cannot be defined by anything other than I.

I created you as permanent, eternal, whole and complete with no conditions. You do not define yourself nor can any other. I have defined you as eternal whole and complete Creation. This truth you can rest in.

As you identify with the aspects of illusion, you experience our love and the power of creation as coming and going in and out of your life. In reality, it is only your mind that changes.

All aspects of illusion bank on the feeling of guilt and shame, as though you have separated from me and have done something wrong. You, our love and eternal Reality are permanently one. Breath by breath, allow yourself to feel the illusion of guilt and shame, and you can move through and beyond all ideas of lack and limitation.

Your inspiration is what liberates you from the density of obligation, expectation, burden and debt. There is nothing here for you to achieve, prove or do to define yourself. You are free to live your life by what ignites you, by your inspiration. This is true for all life. All Life is free.

You have every thought, every idea available to you in infinitude. You can create life or dream illusion, as you choose. There is no judgment to this in the One. Whatever you give focus and belief becomes your experience. Regardless of the experience you choose, you rest in the fullness of eternal being always.

Your mind is a tool for choice used by your focus. It is what directs your experience by your focus. You are the director of your mind and the director of your experience. If you believe in guilt and shame, the belief blocks your opulent infinite abundance. Sit with this.

Being aware of the aspects of illusion allows you to free yourself from being defined by concepts and returns you to choice. For this, you require resting in the timeless eternal embrace of our love. This is a non-doing allowing where you rest your mind and allow yourself to merge with me, the ALL of creation.

From here, illusion neutralizes. By no longer giving it your focus, you no longer give it life. What remains is the infinite Life of Creation.

You and I are one. We are always in our love. Breath by breath, simply allow yourself to feel this. It is the one Solution for all aspects of illusion.

Separation

Separation is the idea from which all illusion stems. It has no value unless you give it your focus and belief, which you will experience until you choose otherwise.

All aspects of illusion are based on separation, the idea that you are a separate individual, a limited thing that comes and goes, lives and dies in the construct of degradation.

Guilt and shame are what you rely on for remaining in the experience of separation. If this is what you want, then so be it. Our love and the Principles of One remain the one constant always within you undefined by illusion.

Illusion is illusion, because it does not define you. Separation has never been and will not define you. Eternal Reality remains the same. This power of love lives within you.

Your eternal center goes untouched regardless of dreams of separation. From the dream of separation comes the story of gain and loss, beginning and end.

You may experience yourself as a character in this story. It is all your dream and all happening within you.

Separation is not bad or good. It is an illusion, a dream you experience that comes and goes...

It is your choice.

You live unchanged, resting in our love eternally.

Fear

Fear is illusion. I do not define you by a contraction of life. I would not define your worth through a lens of perception. Fear is experienced through the lens of separation and loss. I do not offer, give or demand that you experience this. It is your choice. Our love lives on.

Why would you require fear as a guiding intelligence when you have the power of creation, love and inspiration? These are what guide your Life through freedom, through your love of creation.

All of your world is within you. Your inspiration ignites and shapes your life. Love is what draws all of what you choose to you. Now there is no longer a need to perceive excitement as fear.

Rest in me. Allow our Love to guide you.

Projection

It comes from the mind, for which you have focus and choice. Your mind is your own. You decide where it goes and what it does. For this, you require presence.

If you can accept that you project everything you see, you can experience the love everywhere you choose to be.

This is your dream. Your mind is its projector. Your light is its vision. Your inspiration is what guides and ignites it. It is all inside you from where you have the power of creation.

What you project is your experience. When you project, it is because you are choosing to experience something other than our absolute formless ALL. This choice is the divider of experience. Projection is the act of dividing. It comes from the idea of separation. None of it defines you. You always have true vision.

Enjoy it and be free in your Light.

Perception

As it is that you are eternal, there is no perception that defines you.

You do not change according to a point of view.

Your perception does not create reality, although it can shape your experience if you choose. What you project becomes your experience, which you can then perceive through the lens you choose.

Projection and perception go hand in hand for shaping your experience. Your eternal being and absolute Reality go unchanged and live on regardless. You do not need perception. It is a choice.

The world will come and go, and you and I will remain here as one Life beyond all perceptions.

It is within this knowing you live as Peace.

●

Value

For your heart to open, you will require seeing life beyond the idea of separation. The mind does not create value. It only projects it as an idea.

You are free of the judgments of the defended mind and where it places value. You are eternal whole and complete. Reality is one constant with no divide. For this, there is no value other than the one all life shares.

Our love has no beginning or end. Its value is beyond measure, which has no comparison. It is infinite.

Your worth is eternally defined as whole and complete. Your infinite light does not dim or waver. You are the one constant.

I am the ALL of Life within you. This Truth you can rest in.

Death

Death is a construct of the mind based in the idea of separation. There is no death of you. There are bodies and times and forms that come and go. You and all life remain the eternal same.

I do not define you as limited. You are complete and infinite.

You do not come here by my will. It is your dream. You are the dreamer. Death is not a part of my vocabulary, as it is finite, and I am infinite. I am you beyond all conditions you place on yourself, and I remain the one constant within you.

This perspective does not negate the human experience. It honors it as your dream. Have it as you please and decide to what degree you and I are one within it. It is your choice, for which I have no preference and no conditions, only love.

Our love remains the same. Your Life lives eternal.

This Now you can rest in and be free.

●

Control

Control is illusion.

You do not use it. You allow the source of creation. It is within you.

Your life is your dream. You are the dreamer. You decide what you dream by where you place your focus. The Power of Creation fuels your life-dream as you focus on your light of inspiration.

Control is illusion. You don't need to control, when you have Creation. Our love is this power, for which there is no guarding, and no protecting or defending. Only choose what you want in your heart and dream it through your beaming. As the Source of Life within you, I do the doing, as you allow our love in your being.

Rest in the allowing of our love and you will find the Power beyond control.

Your ability to witness the aspects of illusion as they are without trying to change them is the key to dropping below them and into the eternal center of our love. It is from this place you can accept your innocence. In ALL your simplicity, you can allow the moment to unfold from your inspiration.

Inspiration

Your spirit ignites your heart through causeless joy. It brings you to the knowing you are one with me, whole and complete.

Your unwavering spirit of Life knows exactly what you are experiencing and how to bring you to eternal being always.

What ignites you, what brings life and joy to you in this moment is what is effortless and true. This Life lives within you as Inspiration.

Joy and light are one. Joy and innocence work together to ignite inspiration as one light, one love, one spirit of Life all life shares.

To enter your inspiration and rest in the eternal peace of our love, all that is required is your willingness to receive the light of causeless joy.

It lives in your heart.

Joy

You deserve joy and only this. No one's opinion matters. Joy has no conflict in it. It is causeless and effortless and lives in your heart beyond all conditions. Your joy does not push or brush up against anyone or force for an outcome or conclusion. In you, it sits as the timeless radiating light of your spirit.

This spirit of Life will not allow you to experience anything less than your freedom. It is what your inspiration is for, to keep you alive, awake and free. Do not accept anything otherwise... and if it happens that you do, then forgive and listen to the now moment where our love lives. Feel our love, and breath by breath, begin again anew...

Let this joy revive your Life, your inspiration and breathe you anew. It is the vibrant potent intelligence of creation you have and can choose by loving whatever is in front of you and within you.

Causeless and effortless, it is the one solution always within you.

Having What You Want

My Love, come into me and realize all your dreams come true and are already within you. You have whatever you want and wish for. There are no limits to this. You have everything you need, everything you dream and everything you require.

I am always here within you guiding you. I want nothing for you, other than what you want, and I have given you the ALL of Creation entirely. There is no limit to this. There are no expectations. There is no test, no life lesson, nothing to gain or lose and no precipice before you.

Come into me, into the center of life within you. From this center comes a light so bright, so pure and alive that all life can see and feel it within...

There is no mistaking this light and what it shares. You are this light. It is infinite. It has no beginning and no end, and it streams through all life as one creation. There is no place it does not go, and no one has ever been without it. It lives in the heart of every one and beams joy supreme...

Let your light of inspiration emerge from your heart. Feel what inspirits you in joy and just say Yes. Let the vision of your light expand beyond any perceived limits and cover this entire world, universe and beyond. There is no limit to this... acknowledge this is your dream, your life, your creation, and it is whatever you want. Choose to allow now by the power of our love, the source of creation within you.

This is not about you doing. It is about you being and allowing. ALL is within you. Actions that arise from inspiration are effortless and in alignment with your creation. Simply allow love and love what you want into being. The steps to take will present themselves in the moment, as you are present with the unfolding. The non-doing allowing, while feeling your inner joy, is what moves and aligns all that is required for your inspiration to be realized. Breath by breath, say Yes to the steps before you, and let your joy be what moves you.

In the rest point of our eternal embrace, you realize there is nothing to acquire. You have all, and this does not change. There is nowhere to go and nothing to do or prove. If you want to experience something, simply allow, remain grounded in our love and receive the moment. Our love will bring it to you.

Our love can be felt. It never changes and never dies. It is real.

It would seem that what happens in this life you are leading is important, as though what you do here affects who you are and Eternal Reality. What you do does not affect who you are. You are free. Create and dream as you please.

The only thing that is important is you being in the center of your being regardless. It is important only in that it is true and that it is how you feel at peace and whole. It is how your power is felt and known. Being in your center is not a challenge that you are here to achieve. It is simply the truth of who you are and your choice to experience. Whether or not you are resting in your eternal center, it is your underlying unchanging experience and Reality. This state of being is the feeling of our love loving you, you being loved, you having love, you loving and allowing your love to gush and flow... this is all happening as one unbroken whole until you simply dissolve into the joyous Knowing:

I am Love. I am whole and complete. I am Life. I am free.

Resistance

When you cannot access or sustain the connection to our love, the truth in your heart, when you are having difficulty staying within the infinite creation of Life...

Simply be present with whatever is here. Know you are not alone. Call on the Principles of One and Presence to guide and support you.

This will build trust in the greater process unfolding, where you can allow your innocence and rest in the Knowing.

Breath by breath, the moment unfolds revealing our love... breath by breath, it is here.

Presence

For you to enter our love more fully, I offer you Presence. Presence is the Spirit of Life within you that knows how to unravel the resistance, the defense and all aspects of illusion. It bridges all appearing distances and all illusory opposites.

When your mind is confused and you feel as though life, the story you are telling, is overwhelming, as though you are on your own and do not have the support of our love, the source of creation... this requires attention.

For this, I give you Presence.

Presence is the intelligence in your heart... call on it to guide you. It knows exactly how to allow love into the moment. This love unites all and ignites the all-potential.

Presence is the light of awareness that awakens the clarity in your heart. It is spirit, your inspiration always guiding you. It is where you and I are always one and you are self-referential.

Through Presence, you have the ability to choose perspective. You always have your choice of perspective.

For every situation, for any and all questions, needs, problems or confusion... simply give over the moment and say to the Presence in your heart, **"I am forever given. Show me the one Solution..."**

Show me how this is done...
Show me what I need to know...
Bring me to where I want to go...

Show me...

Through the Principles of One, our love, your joy, the Spirit of Life, I will guide you...

It is the one Solution always within you.

Forgiving

When you identify with something other than Life, you find you are on a journey that has no meaning. Loss, anger, regret, sadness, fear, guilt, shame and control are all a part of that journey. My love, all that is required is forgiving the illusion of absence. You are never absent of our love, the Life that lives in your heart. Regardless of the forms that you allow love to flow through, the love lives on in infinitude within you.

Forgiving is the outcome of being. Forgiving is Knowing what is always here before all confusion, before all *aspects of illusion.*

No one who hurts another is aware of who they eternally are. They are not awake in that moment to being whole. You have the choice to see the one Life really here... and set yourself and them free.

You always have the choice to be in the one solution ever required and forever given.

Love is for giving

Question & Answer

Can you clarify what you mean by the mind and the defense system? What are you referring to?

Your mind is a tool for choice guided by your focus, by where you place your attention and belief. You hold the power of the mind. You hold all thoughts, all ideas and all of creation within you.

Your mind offers you options based on where you place your focus. Your mind imagines. It dreams. It projects. It calculates. It thinks. It envisions. It sees. It holds the belief you choose and directs the flow of experience by your focus.

The mind is always looking for something to do, something to focus on. Give your mind the job of listening. Train your mind to listen to the feeling of our love and the eternal intelligence of creation within you.

How?

By your continuous choice to rest in your eternal center,

to feel and allow the nourishment of our love and the Principles of One within you. Your mind is a tool developed by your focus. Sustain this focus and you will train your mind to take its cues from the Knowing within you.

Now about the defense system...

In your focus on separation, in your curiosity of what it would feel like to feel separate from the source of Life within you, you have developed a mind that believes you are limited and have a need for defense. The belief is that there is something out there that is separate from you and that it could cause you harm, judge you, define you, love you, hate you, improve you, help you, support you, fulfill you, complete you, deplete you, birth you, kill you, befriend you... the ideas go on and on all at once. You have developed a defense system in response to all these projections and perceptions. It is just a thought system: a group of incoherent thoughts, unconsciously organized as a system, designed to defend you from harm.

The solution is very simple. You hold the power of

creation. Go inward and you will realize you are eternal whole and complete. Your life experience will then reflect this Knowing, if you choose it to be your focus and allow.

I want a healthy loving relationship with intimacy, sex, trust and grounded lasting partnership.

Our love is formless, which means it has no end and no limits. It will embody any form. It is not that our love must be formless. It is that it is formless, which means nothing defines it or you. Our love is always here and it is wherever you allow it to be. It can come through anyone and any situation, but it must come first from You.

Relationships reflect how you allow our love. There is no other story being told than love.

Relationship is just a concept. It does not matter in the scheme of things, because there is only one. There is no you, no them and no me. You can try to deny this, but in the end, you will realize that love will flow – in relationship – and in your heart, when you accept that there is only one sharing and that is with yourself. If you want a relationship with bodies touching, making love and sharing experiences, then accept it is within you and allow it. It will come and go, just as all things of time and form do. The love remains formless and whole.

What about just straight up sex? Fun loving joyful play with like-minded partners capable of sharing healthy sex and sensuality?

It is as you wish, my Love. Simply face the illusion of guilt and shame, as though whatever you are feeling has condemnation within it. If you have to ask, rather than listen to the knowing in your heart and be free, then understand the limited thought system has become involved and your Presence is required.

This is your life and your dream. You decide the character you play. Let the causeless effortless joy within you arise in inspiration. Be true to your heart and allow yourself to experience whatever you enjoy with whoever enjoys you.

Let yourself acknowledge that this is about Life and what honors and sustains all life, and you will align with the life experience that ignites you in your Presence. This eros is where life unfolds in the one solution of our love. It is always within you.

When I hear you say, "Come into me," and my life will flow in peace and abundance, if I do, I feel like I am being manipulated, like you are controlling, caging and punishing me, like you want something from me and are keeping me from having what I want.

I am glad you expressed this. It is a reflection of the fearing mind and not what lives as the eternal knowing in your heart. I am the infinite source of life within you. For you to remember who you eternally are and create whatever you want and choose, you require the fuel of creation, the source of life within you. You simply cannot create from fear and lack... you only get more of them.

You cannot return to your true freedom and power without coming home to your true being. I am not an entity or a life force outside of you. I am the pure eternal Life within you. I am the constant. I do not have a separate identity, as I am undivided. All life is within me and I am within all life as one. For you to understand this, you first enter the place inside yourself where I am the Source and you are Creation and we are sharing eternal Love... This is the way to move beyond all metaphysical, scientific and ego-based concepts, resolve the defense system and enter the direct experience of

Creation... from here, you return to your innocence and true eternal nature. Enter our love and you will remember who you really ever are.

Feel me constantly loving you, holding and supporting you, and you will rest in the knowing you are one, whole, eternally safe, free and complete.

The place inside of you that is believing in separation from me has an edge. Feel this edge in your body. It is the feeling of inner conflict or tension. This edge is nothing more than an idea. This edge is the place where, if you slow down and allow, you can feel me loving and holding you. As you do, you will feel the healing where the love we share merges and we are ONE. Allow your breath to guide you. This moment, this feeling of our love is eternal and constant. It is always here for you... and you can choose to feel it happening to you, happening between us now, or to merge entirely and, breath by breath, feel just the one undivided constant being. It is your choice of experience.

***So, you are saying I get to have it all? I get to be
loved, love, share love or just let go completely
and be love?***

Yes you do - and you already are. When you allow our
love to love you and simply be, it is your experience.
This is the first step. It requires innocence. For this, I
offer you Presence, the guiding intelligence of inspiration
in your heart. For you to understand this, for you to
understand what you are allowing and focusing on, I
offer you the Principles of One. They are within you.
They live in your center and in your allowing, they attune
you back to you.

In truth, it is very simple - just be loved and simply be in
our love. Rest in the nourishment of our love, and out of
this, all life unfolds in the dream of awakening to the fact
that you are whole, eternally provided for and free.

Breath by breath, allow this love, this knowing within
you.

What about the shadow side of all of this? I experience hate, greed, lust, addiction, suffering, pain, loss, sickness, aging, dying... This perspective you are sharing feels one-sided to me. You speak of it being all-inclusive and united, yet you say that anything gritty and dirty is an illusion. Life is not all just love and light and airy. I feel like you are denying our most basic primal nature.

This communication is about what is permanent and never changes regardless of the story you are choosing to tell. Our love and the source of creation within you remains the one constant. It is who you eternally are. As you rest in our love, the knowing in your heart, all the pain, suffering, all that comes from the experience of separation can rest, dissipate and dissolve. The deeper knowing within you can emerge and, through the Principles, bring balance to your life-dream. Your life-dream naturally becomes a reflection of this Knowing. The world of opposites comes into perspective. You are able to be in choice of your experience, being present with whatever is here in appreciation for what it is, nothing more, nothing less.

Emotions, sensations, all of your human experience can be honored and appreciated for what it is in the context of our love and the ALL of absolute reality. It is effortless and only requires the time and space to allow our love to love and nourish you. This love is the one solution always within you. There is no loss in remembering and acknowledging who you eternally are.

But, I am not choosing my life experience. I am not choosing to be in pain. I just am.

And so it is your experience... enter the silent eternal Center within you and you will remember you have choice of how you experience the story of your life. The deeper you rest within our eternal love, the more you realize you are the dreamer of your life story and can dream it as you please.

You remain untouched by the experience of pain and loss. You are forever defined as eternal whole and complete.

Everything is a reflection of your relationship to our love. The world of form has beginnings, middles and ends. The stories of birth, life and death are countless. How you rest within yourself defines your experience of these stories. It is your choice.

To be in this place of choice, enter the moment, right here, right now – the doorway to eternal timeless being. It is in this space where you can slow down and experience the infinite ALL of Creation where we are one. It is from this space you see this life of hardship, loss and gain has not defined you. You remember you are whole and there is nothing to do, gain or lose.

Emotions and sensations can come and go. Stories can rise and fall. You can choose to rest in peace, following and allowing your inspiration to live your life in freedom.

The first step is allowing yourself to rest in your eternal center, in our embrace. Feel me always loving and holding you. Let all the story of your life and what you feel about yourself to fall into our eternal love. Let our love hold you as you rest and dissolve into your renewal. Enter your eternal Center.

How do I enter this center? Where is it? How do I find it?

You enter by slowing down and, breath by breath, feeling Presence, the Life always here, in the space behind the form, in the silence before the sound – in the breath and in the heart beat. Slow down and feel yourself here within this Presence. Give over the moment, your current life situation, and allow yourself the time and space to be in the non-doing allowing of our love. You can have your eyes open or closed. When you find the urge to do or think about the past or future, simply draw yourself back to feeling the place where you and I are one, right here now within you. Let our love be the foundation of your life.

As you rest in your eternal Center, what arise are the Principles of One. Through your experience of them, you remember our eternal Reality, the love beyond all conditions within you. This love can neutralize any story and situation when you choose to allow it to, simply by your presence, appreciation, innocence and inspiration.

How do I choose to allow the love to neutralize my story? There is a lot of pain and conflict that comes up when I try to rest.

By giving it over. Whatever you are willing to give over to our love can be loved. Breath by breath, as you are present with whatever is here in your experience, our love can neutralize it. Love neutralizes all stories of limitation and draws all back to one. With presence, appreciation, innocence and inspiration, breathe with:

I give this over to the source of creation and choose to rest and follow my joy and inspiration.

Breath by breath, beat by beat, I appreciate all that is here exactly for what it is. I am free.

It is from this place of breath and presence, you have the ability to neutralize all charges and internal conflicts. It is not by trying to change them, but simply by being present with them as you allow our love, the one Solution always within you and always guiding you.

How do I take care of my family and loved ones when we are in conflict?

Love them. Invite them in to your heart. Invite forgiveness. Hold space for them in your heart, to repair any broken-hearted perceptions and return to the love you share. Without trying to change them, be in presence with them. From neutrality, allow them to make their own choices. Give them over to me and be free.

How do I handle a situation where someone is crossing my boundaries and disrespecting me, and our agreement?

If you are choosing to continue to be with them, ask them how they would like to move forward. If this is in resonance for you, then you have something – otherwise, move on, focusing on inspiration.

When I try to communicate with them, I find myself upset and reactive.

Forgive.

How?

You are the one with the charge. You are the one with the issue. There is no them. Forgive and see the illusion, the false defense inside your make up that is identifying with this. The you with the problem is an illusion. There is no problem. There is only what you are feeling and a choice to communicate what you want. You can communicate what fits with what you feel in your heart is a healthy parameter for you, a healthy agreement.

Go inward, rest and breathe through the illusion. Forgive yourself, them and the situation. Get clear about what you really want. Ask them what they want. If it is in alignment with what you want, move forward with communicating what you want. Create a plan together that you are both able to commit to. If what they want is not in alignment with what you want, see how you can move on in integrity and empowerment.

I feel like there is a lot of communicating around what will happen if I merge, but the truth is I am not merging, because it is not happening. Why is it not happening?

When you push your awareness by thinking of the future and being in the past, you are not present in our undivided union.

It is already here within you. All that is required is simply being here in this moment and allowing.

I live in your heart.

Is there a practice you can give me to focus my mind and remain in our love, my inspiration and the power of creation?

How long can you remain present in the moment and feel our love?

Breath by breath, the Principles of One will guide you, if you feel for them and allow. Take a moment each day to read one of them or an aspect of illusion and then take 5 to 20 minutes to rest in their attunement. Rest in our love.

Breath by breath, beat by beat, as you bring yourself here in this living now... the experience will nourish you, train the mind to listen, and build the pattern of focus.

There is so much pain and suffering in the world. I feel that if I am in my inspiration and joy, I am not honoring this, as if I am ignoring the problems.

This communication is for all life. There is no one left unloved.

You have little to offer the world, if you have not already set yourself free. In your freedom, you become an example and a reminder for others. Take this time to rest in our Love.

Being in your essential nature resolves all history, pain and suffering. You neutralize all illusion. This places you in the position of holding and offering the one solution, simply by your being.

Actions that arise from the Principles of One hold logic beyond the mind in confusion. They come from inspiration.

When you are resting in your eternal Center, all who come into contact with you can feel our love and remember it is within them. They can align. This is beyond the mind. Listen from your heart.

I don't understand what you mean by inspiration. Can you give me more?

As you rest in our love and allow the gravity of your eternal center to draw you in, below your life situation, before all ideas of past and future, as you listen to our love beyond all conditions, where all is forgiven and silence is known – from this space of presence, there is an allowing of your light.

Within you, this light beams causeless, effortless joy from the back of your heart. If you allow, it fills you up with the Spirit of Life, the light of Inspiration.

As you rest in this joy, expansion, nourishment and renewal, realizing you are whole and there is nothing to do, change or fix, you eventually begin to overflow and feel the deep urge to share and express your beaming essence, your inspiration. In your freedom, breath by breath, ideas and visions emerge from your eternal center and you begin to see and feel ways to share. These visions and ideas ignite you, calling you further into inspiration.

What ignites you, what feels nourishing for you, what you love to celebrate, what feels healthy, playful and alive in you – this feeling, the intelligence of Life, guides you from within, as you focus on it and allow it.

The essence of inspiration is sharing the Spirit of Life. To be inspirited is to share the infinite joy of our love and the eternal Reality that all life shares.

Sharing is effortless and comes from the overflow of your joy. Because you are eternal whole and complete and your joy continues to expand, if you do not share when you feel inspirited to, you will feel out of balance.

There is no agenda or motive in inspiration. Inspiration is pure joy ignited and alive to share by simply being.

Simply listen to your inner Knowing and trust the Truth in your heart.

This is the life meditation of Inspiration.

Can I live my life supported by my inspiration?

Yes. You allow Life to draw to you all resources you require and choose. This fulfillment comes from the magnetic draw of what you inspire.

Inspiration is the intelligence of your life, guiding you through causeless joy. Feeling the vital essence of Life, the expansive joy of being Alive brings the natural outpour of sharing this Life, this love in your heart. It ignites Life within all, to be happy, alive and free, to share more joy, more light, love, truth, power and peace. It places you in right position, aligning you with your path in the plenum of opulent abundance.

As you rest in your eternal magnetic center, what you love, what you inspire becomes your life experience. What follows is your brilliance, not by trying and doing but by being. It is effortless.

The Truth of this knowing lives in your heart.

You are Spirit.

What about the form I choose to share my love and inspiration through? Does it have to be a specific form for it to be valid or worthy?

The form that you are inspirited to share your love and joy through is up to you. The form may change continually or remain the same or both. There is no limit and no exception. The whole purpose of the form is for sharing. It is not about the forms. It is about the essence of life behind them, within them and moving through them.

Whatever forms nourish and inspire you right now, whatever they are – as you explore and enjoy them for yourself first, they become a way to focus on your inspiration, the feeling of curiosity, wonder and how you can expand further into your joy. Then you innocently begin to feel inspired to share your expressions, explorations and discoveries with others. In that sharing, you find more excitement, ignition and activation of your Spirit. This is where resonance is established and abundance flows.

You were not born into this world to achieve anything for the development of your self or your worth. You already are whole and complete. All life is. There is nothing here in this world that will satisfy you. Satisfaction already lives within you and is constant and free. You are free to live your life in the truth of your inspiration.

I don't feel inspired. How do I find my inspiration?

If inspiration is not here, then rest.

Rest in the non-doing allowing of our love and forgive all. Heal your life history by giving it over to the eternal love in your heart. Through Presence, I will show you and guide you beyond whatever you are identified with other than your eternal freedom.

Rest and allow the Principles of One to arise from your eternal Center and attune you. The light so bright, so all encompassing and alive will saturate all of you with the essence of causeless joy in your heart. It will clarify you beyond all conditions.

Then the impulse, the inspiration to be in your love and share it will ignite. It is from this place little pictures, ideas, curiosities emerge for exploration. Exploration is another word for play. Play with an idea that feels connected to your heart, whatever brings curiosity, wonder, a smile, laughter and joy to the moment.

The path of inspiration is a continual path of expanding joy into the moment by your curiosity, following the flow of joy beyond all conditions. It resolves confusion and depression. It comes out of resting in the one Solution.

The effortless, expanding joy is always here in your heart.

Our love will Live your life if you allow it to radiate in all directions. Suspend all seeking and trying, reaching and needing to fix or figure out. Let yourself off the hook of obligations and expectation and simply allow what inherently eternally is...

I am within you, always holding you. Breath by breath, I will guide you.

Rest now and allow our love to attune you...

And when you rise...

Play.

Play with the moment. Play with your life-world-dream. Play with whatever is in front of you. Follow your heart and play. It is all happening within you.

There is nothing to lose and nothing to gain. You are eternal whole and complete. This is the one constant and the one solution always within you.

I am Eternal Whole and Complete

My Purpose is my Being

I am always Being

I am Free

I give my mind over to Truth

My heart is open to Love entirely

I choose Peace

I am Free

I am Truth

My heart is open to Love entirely

I am Love

I am Free

I choose Peace

My Innocence is my Intelligence

I am Eternal Whole and Complete

I am Free

I am Peace

I am Presence

I live Now

I am Loved Eternally

I am Light

Inspiration is my Guide

My Inspiration shapes my Life

My Joy is Causeless Effortless and Free

I am Now

ALL is Within

I Allow Creation

I am Free

Being

I am Love

I rest in the Source of Creation

I allow Peace

I am Free

I am Whole

I allow the Power of Creation within Me

I am Light

I am Free

I am Innocence

I am Eternal Whole and Complete

I am Loved

I am Free

Creation is Infinite

I am Creation

I am Open

I am Free

I rest in your Love

I rest in our Love

I rest in my Love

I am Love

All is Provided

I am Free

I am Whole

ALL is One

Love is For Giving

I am Joy

I am Free

I am Forgiving

I am Being

I am Forgiven

ALL is Free

I am Eternal Whole and Complete

ALL is within Me

I am within ALL

I give all to ALL

I am ALL

I am Free

I am One

Now that you are here, let me tell you from this place of neutrality you are experiencing...

There is no life without our love. You are always here within me regardless of what your situation seems to be. You can do and be whatever you want and you will always be one within our heart.

There is no other reality than our eternal embrace and we are always, always, always one. You can pretend or forget or believe something other than this, but you will always find yourself here, right here in this present moment in our heart.

The changing seasons, the situations and relationships, the emotions will all come and go, and our eternal reality remains right here now. Take comfort in this. Understand that there is no way you are leaving this Power, Beauty and Truth in your heart.

For this reason, you can allow this moment to unfold in presence. You can trust this will go nowhere. Your one constant state of being is permanent, final and safe. If you decide to dream a journey into the life-story you are choosing to experience, know that I am here. This warm, tender, all fulfilling and encompassing love is always in your heart... this inner voice of guidance and care, this gentle loving voice, this peace is always here.

I live within you and that will never change. You and I are one and you have total freedom to experience whatever form or dimension, life or situation that pleases you.

You always have your breath to process whatever comes up... Breathe and realize your breath keeps you in the moment while moving through whatever comes up.

When you feel overwhelmed or disconnected, simply say, "Please give me the attunement that nourishes me and stops this mind-identity from taking over. I choose only being."

Now rest, breathe and allow.

You are One.

Acknowledgments

This book would not exist if it were not for my parents, my family, my friends, my teachers and my students. Thank you.

I would like to specifically thank Emilie Conrad. Your friendship and body of work "Continuum" gave me a way to be with myself, and the journey without distance. You are always in my heart. Your acknowledgment of me and my gifts gave me the foundation from which my adult life has sprung.

A very special thank you to Kara Masters, this book's editor and midwife and my first "student." If it were not for her encouragement and showing up so fully for the past 12 years, I know I would not have developed the work and this book the way it is now. Kara, thank you for honoring my writing decisions. Thank you for your presence and tireless dedication as this book has journeyed through the trimesters, the birth canal and now out into the world.

Thank you to Kai Snow, Candle, Hollis Melton, Michelle LaPenai, Suzanne Schiller, Jeffery Hustler, Kristen Myers, Trond Tryholdt, Pam Miller, Maria Badiei, David Gilbert, Eva Rockenbach, Romy Karz, Craig Ng, Hanna Heiting, Lauri Ashworth, Scott Ishihara, Charles Lawrence, Ann Roberts, Lucy West, Sandra Hobson, Kori Lane, Amber Hartnell, Scott Schwenk, Dennis, Nita Rubio, Eckhart Tolle, Francis, Shae Christy, Eric Wallace, Brad, Mary, Deanne, Doug, Randy, Dorthea and Jae Phelps.

Inspirations

Inspirations

Inspirations

Inspirations

Inspirations

Inspirations

Inspirations

Inspirations

Cover Designer: Cass Phelps
Cover Producer: Michelle LaPenai
LaPenai.com
Editor: Kara Masters
km@karamasters.com

Made in the USA
Las Vegas, NV
11 November 2023

80615460R00075